MIKE POWER'S

DORSET TEASHOP WALKS

Introduction

I have written several circular walk guides but this book is a new departure for me. Whilst taking afternoon tea at the recently restored Highcliffe Castle, the proprietor suggested I might like to consider writing a guide to circular teashop walks. After a little research I have completed ten in the south-eastern corner of the county, which range from 2 - 5 miles. The furthest point west is Upwey near Weymouth, in the south it is Kimmeridge in the Purbeck Hills whilst Highcliffe is the furthest east close to the Hampshire border.

Dorset is a beautiful county attracting visitors from all over the world. It is easy to see why having a mild climate, 75 miles of stunning coastline and numerous picture postcard villages. What could be nicer on a summer's day than an enjoyable walk followed by afternoon tea. I enjoyed all these walks I hope you will too.

© Power Publications
1 Clayford Ave
Ferndown.
Dorset. BH22 9PQ

ISBN 1898073 24 4

Other local Dorset publications
Pub Walks in Dorset
40 More Pub Walks in Dorset
Pub Walks in Hardy's Wessex
The Dorset Coast Path
A Mountain Bike Guide to Dorset
Dorset Pilgrimages
A Century of Cinema in Dorset
Mike Power's Pub Walks Along the Dorset Coast

Publisher's note
Whilst every care has been taken to ensure that all the information contained in this book is correct neither the authors or publishers can accept any responsibility for any inaccuracies that may occur.

Front cover: Old post office tearooms. Organford.

Walk	Location	Miles	Page
1	Bockhampton	2¼	4
2	Gotham	3	6
3	Highcliffe	2	11
4	Kimmeridge	5	13
5	Milton Abbas	2½	17
6	Organford	5	20
7	Pamphill	2¾	22
8	Shillingstone	3¼	24
9	Upwey	3½	27
10	Wareham	3½	29

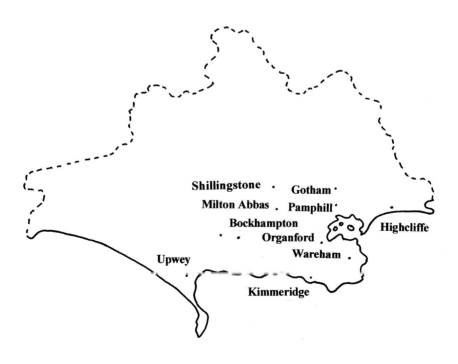

Bockhampton - Pine Lodge Farm Tearooms.

Pine Lodge Farm is located off the Stinsford road a short distance from the roundabout at the eastern end of the Dorchester by-pass. If approaching from the east on the A35 take the turning before the bridge sign-posted to Higher and Lower Bockhampton then turn left at the crossroads. Ample parking in front of tearooms and in the large field opposite.

These beautifully kept tearooms occupy a peaceful position well away from the lane. Outside are picnic benches beside a small orchard and aviary containing a splendid owl. Opening times summer Wednesday - Saturday lunches 12 - 2 cream teas and snacks all day. Sundays roast 12 - 2, cream teas 3 - 5.30. Winter times Sunday only 12 - 2.30. Tel: 01305 266 052

Approximate distance: 2¼ miles. OS maps: Outdoor Leisure 15 and Landranger 194 728/918.

A very scenic and enjoyable walk at first on farm paths and tracks in the Frome Valley then on heath and woodland paths high up on to Duddle Heath where Hardy's Cottage is located. Attractive field and woodland paths descend gently back to the tearooms.

From the tearooms go back down to the lane, cross to the track opposite walking down as far as the finger post by the dwelling at which point turn left. Path sign-posted, Norris Mill ¾. Walk between dwellings to the stile and keep straight ahead on the raised grass path until you reach the stile on the right. Cross into the field and make your way over to the stiles and plank bridge opposite maintaining direction over a pair of stiles and the field ahead. After two more stiles and a plank bridge bear left up the field to the gate, along the track, beside the barn and dwelling, and up to the road.

Cross to the stile opposite and keep straight ahead on the field path to reach the stile in the far boundary then follow the woodland path beyond which bears right down to the junction of two paths. Immediately climb the stile on the left and join the narrow, undulating heath and woodland path which winds its way gently up to a cross track. Turn left and continue following the path through the pine wood, occasionally marked by yellow tipped posts. The path continues to rise through rhododendron bushes, at one point crossing a track after which it rises fairly steeply through a birch wood before joining the Roman road at the top then turn left.

The route back is on the left beyond the stile, sign-posted Bockhampton but a short de-tour ahead will take you the ¼ mile down to Hardy's Cottage. Before dropping back to Bockhampton a red arrow on the right directs you down a short path to Rushy Pond - a haven for wildlife. Keep straight ahead on this pleasant holly-lined track which descends gently to a finger post then turn left to the stile sign-posted, to Lower Bockhampton. Enjoying good views over the Frome Valley and hills beyond keep to this well-surfaced grass path which leads directly back to the tearooms.

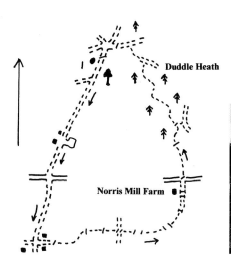

Duddle Heath

Norris Mill Farm

Gotham - The Heavy Horse Centre Tearooms.

An opportunity to combine a visit to the Heavy Horse Centre with a lovely walk. Best time of the year is in May when there are masses of bluebells to be seen. The centre is located north of Verwood and can be reached from the B3081 or the B3078.

Open 10 - 5 from the end of March until the end of October (or when the half term holiday falls) the present charges are £4-95 for adults and £2-95 for children. There is a car park at the centre but if you are walking before visiting the centre it would be courteous to tell them. In addition to heavy horses they have miniature ponies and donkeys, llamas, pygmy goats, kune kune pigs and baby lambs to feed. Tel: 01202 824040

Approximate distance: 3 miles. OS maps Landranger 195 and Outdoor Leisure 22 079/088.

This extremely enjoyable walk in this very peaceful area of Dorset can be muddy but not over demanding. Commencing along a lovely old unmade bluebell-lined green lane you soon join a bridleway passing between beautiful bluebell woods which guides you to the village of Edmondsham with an opportunity to visit the house and gardens. A ¾ mile walk along a peaceful lane and a field path delivers you back to the centre.

Go back through the entrance gates and immediately take the track on the left, (an old County green road) which shortly veers to the left dropping steadily beneath a hazel canopy. It is very attractive, fringed with bluebells and other wild flowers but often wet underfoot especially in the winter months. Ignore the footpath on the right but keep to the track which bears left then crosses a small bridge over the River Crane beyond which the track is dotted with primroses, bluebells and patches of garlic ransoms. Further ahead on the left is Great Rhymes Copse, a lovely large bluebell wood.

At the junction with the bridleway bear left passing yet another small beautiful bluebell wood on the right. All the way along the track both sides are lined with masses of bluebells which give way to garlic ransoms as it rises gently uphill.

At the top look for a sign-posted bridleway on the left and take this path which rises through a beech wood to meet a track at the top. Turn left, walk for a while then turn right at the cross track, which takes you down to the village of Edmondsham.

Turn right if you want to visit Edmondsham House and garden otherwise turn left. Follow this peaceful undulating lane and after crossing a bridge and passing the thatched cottage take the sign-posted footpath on the left at the bottom of a short track. (Alternatively you can stay on the lane but the road after the junction carries some fast moving traffic). Beyond the stile the fenced path rises along the edge of a field, up to another stile and into a second. Bearing slightly right walk up the field to a stile in the opposite hedge then maintain direction making for one last stile in the right-hand hedge. Turn right retracing your steps back to the centre.

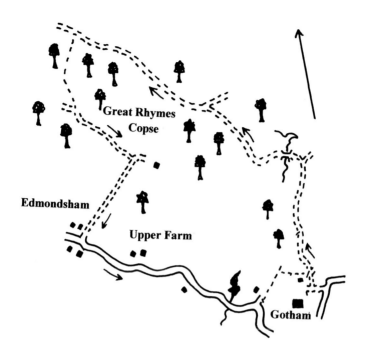

Great Rhymes Copse

Edmondsham

Upper Farm

Gotham

Walk No. 2

Great Rhymes Copse

Walk No. 2

Highcliffe Castle Tearooms.

The castle is in Rothesay Road, Highcliffe signed from the A327 Lymington Road. Car park charges apply from 1st April - 30 September. Tearooms open mid morning to mid afternoon, all year round, 10am - 5pm in summer. Tel: 01425 270924

This Grade 1 listed castle has been recently restored having laid derelict for many years following a disastrous fire. It is now open to the public with a visitor centre containing an exhibition of the history and its owners. Entrance fee is usually £1-50, children free when accompanied.

Approximate distance: 2 miles. OS maps Landranger 195 and. Outdoor Leisure 22. 203/932.

A short but very enjoyable scenic seaside stroll, not over strenuous ideal for all the family.

From the castle car park head southwards following the path which zig-zags down to the front at which point turn left. Excellent views of the Needles are afforded across the Solent from this well surfaced path which runs the length of the beach before reaching the stream at Chewton Bunny.

Head inland only as far as the steps on the left, climb them and follow the path which forks right up to the car park.

Keep to the path on the cliff edge until you can go no further then go down the steps on the left and turn right onto the undercliff path. Further on fork right and when the path divides keep to the higher of the two which eventually drops down to a lower track. Take the next right fork and before reaching the beach climb the steps back to the castle grounds for an enjoyable pot of tea.

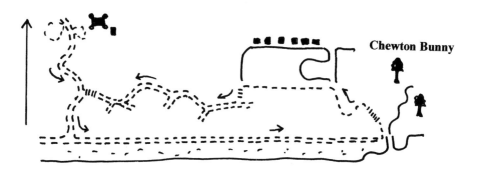

Chewton Bunny

Kimmeridge Post Office & Tearooms.

Leave the A351, Wareham by-pass and follow the Kimmeridge signs south. The post office and tearooms are on the left as you enter the village. Opening times daily 9 - 5.30. There is a small car park at the tearooms, a free park on the left as you descend the hill towards Kimmeridge but the large main car park is accessed via the tollgate. Present fee is £2. Tel: 01929 480701

Kimmeridge lies on the Dorset Coast Path and is one of the county's most unspoilt villages despite the fact that the area is rich in natural oil. A 'nodding donkey' on the cliff has been producing oil every day for as long as I can remember. There are also vast quantities of bituminous shale which the Romans turned into jet-like jewellery.

Approximate distance: 5 miles. OS maps. Outdoor Leisure 15 and Landranger 195 918/798.

Very scenic but slightly demanding this bracing walk follows the Dorset Coast Path as far as Rope Lake Head then heads inland steeply up onto Swyre Head (one of the best view points in the Purbeck hills) returning along Smedmore Ridge.

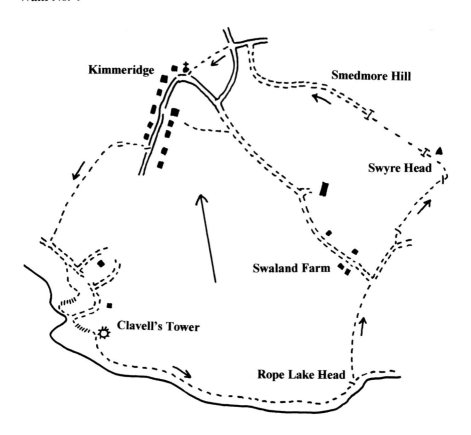

Leave the tearooms turning left towards the coast and just past the last cottage on the right climb the stile into the field walking to the stiles and bridge on the far side then turn left, sign-posted Kimmeridge Bay 1 mile. Upon reaching the tarred road turn left, go across to the corner of the car park, through to the next car park and join the sign-posted footpath on the right. Descend the steps, go through the boatyard and straight ahead up the steps on to Hen Cliff. The Rev. John Richards who inherited Smedmore House and estate in 1817 built the folly Clavell's Tower in 1831. The Clavell family who lived here came to England with the Conqueror.

Walk for a mile and a half along this attractive section of coast until you reach the stile on the left at Rope Lake Head then head inland to the top of the field. Two options: For a less demanding walk turn left onto the gravel track. After passing through Swalland Farm the track merges with a tarred road passing Smedmore House. Keep walking until you finally reach a stile on the left then bear right across the field in the direction of the waymark to the stile in the boundary keeping straight ahead to a couple more stiles before reaching the café.

For the more energetic and a more scenic walk keep straight ahead up the track (permitted path) and where it bears right, cross to the stile on the left. The path is not well defined but pick your way up keeping as close as possible to the wire fence on the right. Take care, as it is steep in places and a bit overgrown near the top. Eventually you come to a stile, which allows access to Swyre Head. It is a wonderful scenic spot with views of Chapman's Pool to the east and Kimmeridge Bay to the west. Encombe House can be seen in the valley behind.

Continue heading west along the ridge of Smedmore Hill, past the trig point and through the gate onto the bridleway. Further on pass through the small gate (Heavens Gate) and keep to the track ahead eventually dropping down to the lane. Turn left and carefully walk to the junction, crossing to the stile opposite. The field path drops down to the village to the left of the church.

Clavell's Tower

Milton Abbas Tea Clipper Tearooms

Milton Abbas is signed from the A345 at Milbourne St Andrews. The charming thatched tearooms are open Wednesday to Sunday 10.30 - 5.30 also Bank Holidays. Tel: 01258 880223

Milton Abbas is probably one of the most photographed villages in Dorset nearly all the residents living in pretty thatched cottages. The village was originally built close to the abbey buildings but in the 18th century the then earl built the present houses and moved the population into them as he felt their existing homes spoilt the view from his mansion. The church was part of a Benedictine monastery. St Catherine's Chapel hidden in the woods above the abbey grounds was once a place of pilgrimage.

Approximate distance of walk: 2½. miles. OS maps: Explorer 117 and Landranger 194. 805/018.

There are two options for the first section of this walk. The most scenic follows a path beside Milton Lake leading to Milton Abbey but means a short walk along the often busy road which has no pavements. The other takes you up through the village to join a bridleway leading to a quiet residential road and track beyond. Both routes lead to the chapel beyond where a rising track passes through attractive woods with numerous garlic ransoms and bluebells. The final section follows a field path boundary before dropping down through a small wood. Hilly in places but not over demanding this very scenic walk is ideal for all the family.

Option 1. From the tearooms walk down through the village turning right at the bottom, cross the road and walk until you reach the signposted footpath on the left. Known as the monk's path it skirts the lake before reaching a path junction. Continue ahead to visit the abbey otherwise turn right. Although not an official right of way it is a permissive path but in the school holidays when the house is open an entrance fee is charged. Follow the path past the grass staircase on the right, which leads to the chapel but no longer open to the public.

Turn right when you reach the entrance, go out into the road and turn right again. Keeping to the right-hand side pass under the grass-stepped bridge walking up the hill for a short distance then cross over to join the gravel track on the left.

Almost immediately take the footpath on the immediate left through a young beech wood following up to and round the chapel. Continue on the main path where in late May the air is scented from the numerous garlic ransoms. It rises to meet a cross track, keep walking left through a lovely area of bluebells eventually reaching the cross track at the top.

Turn right through the gatehouse entrance and join the sign-posted bridleway on the right which eventually reaches a gate. Pass through bearing left across the field to a similar gate and out to the road. Turn left and in a few paces take the grass-surfaced bridleway on the right running between the dwellings to meet a road. Turn right then immediately left into the cul-de-sac making your way to the right-hand corner to pick up a section of the Jubilee Trail. This wide stepped path drops you directly down to the road at the top of Milton Abbas

Option 2. From the tearooms walk back up through the village, past the school and join the sign-posted bridleway on the left. Stepped in places it rises through a small wood to a cul-de-sac and out into an estate road. Turn left and keep walking as tarmac gives way to gravel then drops down to meet two paths on the right close to the road. Take the one on the left which leads to the chapel after which continue following option 1 at the third paragraph.

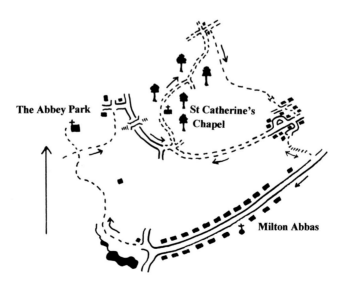

St Catherine's Chapel

Organford - Old Post Office Tearooms.

Organford is sign-posted both from the A35 and A351 west of Lychett Minster. The attractive tearooms, previously the post office are open daily 11.30 - 5.30 from Wednesday through to Monday. Weekends 12.30 - 6. Tel: 01202 622440

Approximate distance: 5 miles. OS maps: Landranger 195 and Outdoor Leisure 15 923/940.

A mostly level peaceful walk on wide forest tracks and attractive woodland paths with just a few short road sections. There are no stiles and for the most part the surface is generally good underfoot.

From the entrance of the tearooms turn left over the bridge and immediately join the track on the right walking as far as Bridge Cottage then take the track on the right sign-posted, Sherford Bridge 1¼ miles. Maintain direction through the gate and follow the wild flower-lined track ahead. For about half a mile after entering the wood keep walking until you reach the large wide gravel track and turn left.

Dotted beside the track are ponds home to dragonflies and other aquatic wildlife. Maintain direction for just over a mile and where the track veers to the right bear left in to the nature reserve keeping to the well trodden path across the heath eventually reaching a small housing development. Go round to the left, straight ahead at the junction following the road up, round and down to the bend then join the footpath on the left leading to the road.

Turn left, walk a few steps then carefully cross over into Keysworth Drive walking as far as the Labour Club then join the footpath on the left behind the dwellings which leads to an attractive wood. Cross the bridge by the brook and keep straight ahead until you eventually reach the road then turn left and walk up to the crossroads.

Cross into the road opposite, walking past Sandford Park and after the Claypipe Inn take the next track on the left. Go down as far as the gate and turn right forking right at the track retracing your steps back to the tearooms.

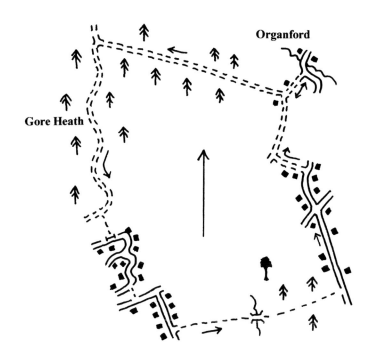

Organford

Gore Heath

Pamphill Dairy Tearooms

The delightful village of Pamphill, once part of the Bankes Estate but now belonging to The National Trust, is signposted from the B3082 Wimborne to Blandford road. The tearooms which adjoin Pamphill Dairy shop are open daily 10 - 5. Tel: 01202 880618

Approximate distance: 2¾ miles. OS: maps Landranger 195 and Explorer 118. 995/003.

Chocolate box thatched cottages and period houses abound along this extremely enjoyable walk ideal for all members of the family which first follows a scenic path beside the River Stour returning along an attractive, gently rising bridle track.

Leave the entrance to the tearooms, cross to the gravel track opposite walking to reach the green. Keep straight ahead out onto the road by the school, past the Vine Inn, a good refreshment stop, and down to the junction at the bottom of Vine Hill.

Cross to the squeeze stile and bear right, over a couple more stiles turning left towards the river to pick up the very attractive path on the right. Keep walking until you reach a stile and gate then turn right and join the slightly sunken woodland path following it for some distance, cross the bridge and walk up to the road.

Turning left, cross over towards Poplar Farm and join the sign-posted bridleway on the left. Keep to this grass and gravel track until you reach the cottages at 1 New Road and just before the lane turn right onto the bridleway sign-posted 'All Fools Lane'. This very attractive, well surfaced, sunken fern-lined track rises steadily but gently, through a couple of gates before reaching the lane at the top at which point turn right, past St Peter's church back to the tearooms.

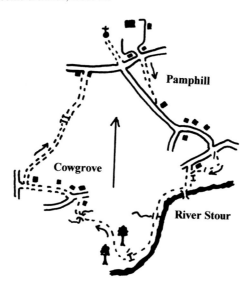

The River Stour

Walk No. 8
Shillingstone - The Willows Tearooms.

Village on the A357 just over a mile north from Durweston. Tearooms are on the right. Opening times everyday except Monday between 10 and 6 (5 in the winter) Closed from Christmas until the first weekend in February then open weekends only until March. Parking at tearooms also space in side roads close by. Tel: 01258 861167

Approximate distance: 3¼ miles. OS maps: Explorers 118/129 and Landranger 194 832/106.

A very enjoyable walk which twice crosses the River Stour and passes through the hamlets of Hanford and Little Hanford. Whilst mostly flat it can sometimes be very wet when the river is high.

Turning left out of the tearooms and for safety sake cross the road and in a few paces carefully cross back into Holloway Lane. Walk to the gates at the bottom and bear right across the field to the bridge. On the far side turn immediately left walking to the gate, up the short track then go through the small gate into the hazel coppice on the left.

Follow the narrow twisting path until you reach the gate on the right, cross the field to the gate on the far side then turn right and pass through the gate on the left. Keep straight ahead past the farm buildings, through three more gates before reaching the lane at Hanford.

Turn left, walk up and round the lane turning left at the entrance to Hanford School and in 25 paces join the sign-posted footpath on the left. Walk to the stile, cross the track to the gate keeping straight ahead beside the hedge crossing into the field on the right when you reach the gate. Head up the field bearing left at the top, around the fence and across to the stile in the far boundary.

Turn left down the bridleway to the gate at the bottom, go through into the field and bear right across to the gate opposite then bear left across the meadow to the footbridge. Cross to the far bank then bear left up to the stile and over the dis-used railway line, walking to the stile at the top of the field and turn right. Almost immediately go left over the stile and follow the scrub-land path up to another stile turning right into the lane leading to the main road.

Turn left then carefully cross over into Everetts Lane following the footpath ahead signed, to Wessex Ave. Ignore the first footpath on the right but continue along the lane and take the next one which is sign-posted across a plank bridge. Head up and across the field to the stile on the far side keeping straight ahead past 'The Cottage' turning right along the lane. Continue past several dwellings until you reach the signed bridleway on the left which drops straight back down to the road opposite the tearooms.

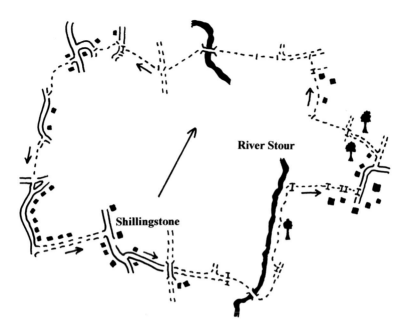

River Stour

Shillingstone

The River Stour - Shillingstone

Upwey - Wishing Well Café

Village signposted off the A354 Dorchester to Weymouth road at Elwell.
Tearooms are open daily 10.30 - 6, March 1st. _ Mid December (closed Monday and Tuesday in March, Oct, Nov and Dec) Entry is free to the beautiful water gardens at the rear which also allows access to the well, source of the River Wey. Tel: 01305 814470

Approximate distance: 3½ miles. OS maps: Landranger 194 and Outdoor Leisure 15. 661/853.

Hilly at first and slightly demanding this scenic ramble takes you across Friar Waddon Hill then after following a long track, level field paths guide you back south of the village.

Start from the café and go up the drive at the side to the stile following the steep track beyond, up through the copse (can be slippery in places when wet). Climb the stile at the top and keep straight ahead across the field to the gate on the far side. Maintain direction to one last stile walking until you reach the tarred lane.

Turn left keeping to this very peaceful track, downhill between fields then up the far hill which then bears left to meet a cross track at which point turn left.

Upon reaching the dwelling on the right look for a signed footpath on the left leading to a plank bridge, cross into the field and turn right walking round until you see the

stiles in the hedge. Climb into the field and immediately pass through the gate into the field on the left then turn right walking to the crossing point in the far hedge. Fork left in the direction of the left-hand waymark on the stile heading for the bend in the field allowing access to the small field behind the hedge. Walk close to Pucksey Brook soon to reach a bridge taking you to the opposite bank.

Keeping to the left-hand hedge walk up the field making for the stiles and plank bridge in the far boundary then bear right up to the stile beside the metal gate. Cross the track to the gate opposite and go straight ahead down the field to the stile following the track ahead close to Westbrook House. Turn left walking the length of the village back to the tearooms.

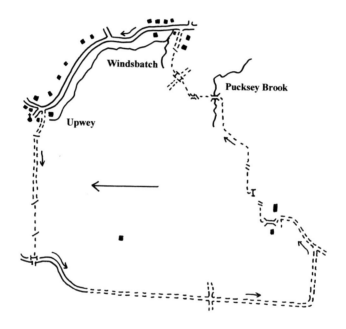

Wareham - The Old Granary.

The Old Granary is located next to the River Frome right on the quay. Turn off the A351 at the southern end of town. Public 'pay & display' car parks on the quay and by the church. Cream teas served 2.30 - 5.30, lunch 12 - 2.30, morning coffee 10 - 12 and the restaurant is open 6 - 9.30. Tel: 01929 552010

Approximate distance: 3½ miles. OS maps: Landranger 195 and Outdoor Leisure 15. 925/872.

A peaceful, level walk which takes you down to Swinham Point returning on a narrow undulating river path beside the Frome. During the summer months wildflowers abound among the reeds which attract large numbers of butterflies and other insects. Although the riverside path is cleared on a regular basis on some occasions you may find some areas are overgrown. It can also be wet when the river is high usually only in the winter.

From The Old Granary turn right, pass through the gap in the corner of the car park after which turn right again across Church Green then left in front of the church. Take the next right following this tarred drive down between the cemetery and turn left at the fingerpost. Walk for a while then climb the bank onto the old town wall, cross the road and rejoin the next section of wall.

Walk for awhile then look for a path on the right (opposite a road to a housing development). Go down to the tarred drive and turn left. All along the route are clumps of prickly Butcher's Broom. Pass through both kissing gates either side of the track to the quarry and just before the dwelling fork left onto the track following it until it bears left to a stile.

Stay close to the woodland strip on the right eventually reaching a bridge then maintain direction keeping to the well-beaten path around the edge of the fields finally arriving at a stile. Cross to the narrow grass strip following it round to metal crossing point. From here the route needs little or no explanation. The path is very undulating following the meandering course of the river and at times can be wet and become overgrown prior to summer cutting. Often the only sounds are that of waterfowl or the reeds blowing gently in the wind.

Keep walking until directed inland across a board walk and footpath, beyond which fork left out to the track behind the church then simply take the next left and retrace your footsteps back to the start.

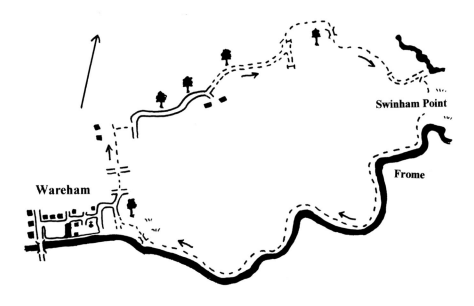

River Frome

Walk No. 10